Crime and Punishment

Kathy Elgin

Author: Kathy Elgin
Illustrator: Adam Hook

First American edition published in 2005 by
Compass Point Books
3109 West 50th Street, #115
Minneapolis, MN 55410
Visit Compass Point Books on the Internet at *www.compasspointbooks.com* or e-mail your
request to *custserv@compasspointbooks.com*

© 2005 by Compass Point Books

First published in Great Britain by
Cherrytree Books (a member of the Evans Publishing Group)
2A Portman Mansions
Chiltern Street
London W1U 6NR, United Kingdom
Copyright © Bailey Publishing Associates Ltd.
This edition published under license from Evans Brothers Limited

Library of Congress Cataloging-in-Publication Data
Elgin, Kathy
   Crime and punishment : Changing times / written by Kathy Elgin.
      p. cm—(Changing times)
   Includes bibliographical references and index.
   ISBN 0-7565-0885-1 (hardcover)
   1. Shakspeare, William, 1564-1616—Characters—Criminals—Juvenile literature. 2.
Crime—England—History—16th century—Juvenile literature. 3. Crime—England—
History—17th century—Juvenile literature. 4. Criminals in literature—Juvenile literature.
5. Criminals—England—Juvenile literature. 6. Crime in literature—Juvenile literature. I.
Hook, Adam, ill. II. Title. III. Changing times (Minneapolis, Minn.)
   PR3026.E44 2004

   822.3'3—dc22   2004025340

Contents

Introduction

Who Was Shakespeare?

William Shakespeare is probably the most famous playwright in the world. He was born in 1564 in Stratford-upon-Avon, and 400 years after his death his plays are still being performed all over the world in almost every language you can think of. Although he came from a fairly ordinary family and didn't even go to college, he wrote 38 plays with exciting plots and new, dramatic language.

Most of his plays were performed at the Globe, one of the very first theaters in London. Some were also performed for Queen Elizabeth I herself at court. Because he was also an actor and probably appeared in some of his own plays, Shakespeare knew what audiences liked. He became one of the most popular playwrights of his day, and by the time he died in 1616, he was a wealthy man.

Crime and Punishment in Shakespeare's Time

There was a lot of crime in Elizabethan England during the Renaissance era. Part of the problem was poverty. There were no social services in those days, and many people were forced to steal money or food simply to stay alive. But it was also due to the way Elizabethans thought about society. They liked a calm and settled way of life, which depended on everyone behaving themselves and being content to remain in their own proper places.

Most people lived their whole lives in the village or town where they were born and worked for the local landowner. They were very suspicious of strangers, especially if they were poor or unemployed. Anyone who disturbed the peace was considered a threat to society and had to be punished. Homeless people and beggars in particular were regarded as criminals, even if they had not committed any particular crime.

Crimes like murder and treason were, of course, very serious and deserved proper punishment. Many people, however, were punished harshly for things that we consider quite trivial—stealing bread, perhaps, or just being out on the street at night. There were a lot of complicated laws and a wide range of quite brutal punishments, some of which seem more like torture to us.

Shakespeare had seen beggars wandering the countryside when he lived in Stratford. When he moved to London he saw pickpockets and other thieves in the streets. All these types of people found their way into his plays.

Vagrants, Beggars, and Outcasts

Vagrants, or vagabonds, were people who had no home or job. They wandered about the countryside, surviving by begging for food and money. They were usually servants who had been let go, or wounded soldiers unable to work. There were also orphan children and women deserted by their husbands. People were afraid of beggars because they often traveled in large groups and sometimes became violent.

Disabled beggars got more sympathy. Some had genuine war wounds, but others injured themselves—or their children—on purpose.

> *... like silly beggars*
> *Who, sitting in the stocks, refuge their shame,*
> *That many have and others must sit there.*
> RICHARD II, ACT 5, SCENE 5

silly: simple, defenseless
refuge: shelter from

The law said that poor people had to be supported by the church. Nobody wanted to pay to support vagrants, of course, so local residents always wanted them to move on. But before that, they had to be punished. The penalty for begging was to be put in the stocks and then tied to the back of a cart and whipped out of town. Police officers went around the streets at night, looking in all the taverns for homeless people. All those who could not prove that they had a home were rounded up and brought to court in the morning.

what I do, to spite the world.

People came out onto the street to watch and jeer as vagrants were whipped out of town.

... I am one, my liege,
Whom the vile blows and buffets of the world
Hath so incens'd, that I am reckless what
I do, to spite the world.
MACBETH, ACT 3,
SCENE 1

liege: lord
buffets: knocks
incens'd: angered
reckless: careless

The person most feared was the "masterless man," one who had no job and no respect for the law. They often appear in plays and are called "malcontents." In real life they were outcasts from society and often were forced to become criminals. The man who speaks here is someone to whom so many terrible things have happened that he no longer cares what dreadful deeds he does to get back at the world. Because of this, he has agreed to commit a murder for Macbeth.

Society was very divided, with a huge gap between rich and poor.

Thieves and Robbers

There was a whole underworld of professional criminals. They even had their own language, a kind of slang called "Peddlar's French." A "nipper" cut off purses from people's belts. A pickpocket was called a "foist," "priggers of prancers" were horse thieves, and "coney-catchers" were swindlers who tricked people out of their money. The crowded city streets swarmed with these rogues. An Italian visitor to London wrote, "There is no country in the world where there are so many thieves and robbers as in England . . . ."

> ... he daily doth frequent
> With unrestrained loose companions,
> Even such, they say, as stand in narrow lanes
> And beat our watch and rob our passengers.
>
> RICHARD II, ACT 5, SCENE 3

frequent: associate
loose: immoral
passengers: travelers, passers-by

Pickpockets only stole money or handkerchieves. They rarely attacked anyone violently.

Bolingbroke is talking about his young son Hal, the future King Henry V, who is involved with bad company. In the narrow streets, mugging was common, especially after dark. Gangs of men hung about waiting to set upon unwary travelers or drunks returning late from the tavern. Nervous citizens could hire a "linkboy" with a torch to light them safely home. In the countryside, highwaymen were a constant danger.

> Alas, what danger will it be to us,
> Maids as we are, to travel forth so far?
> Beauty provoketh thieves sooner than gold.
>
> AS YOU LIKE IT, ACT 1, SCENE 3

Above: *Nicholas Jennings was a notorious coney-catcher, who would disguise himself both as a ragged beggar and a respectable citizen.*

Women traveling alone were particularly at risk. Rosalind and Celia decide that one of them should dress as a boy for safety on their journey to the Forest of Arden. A relatively harmless trick was for vagrants to hold up rich people and steal their clothes. They then dressed them in their own rags, made their getaway, and later sold the good clothes for money. This is one of the comic scenes in *The Winter's Tale.*

Highwaymen held people up at gunpoint and shot those who resisted. Because of this, they were hanged when caught.

Murderers

Murder has always been considered the worst of all crimes. It was punishable by death, usually by hanging. Murders in the course of robbery were common. Elizabethan constables often found bodies in the street in the morning. But Shakespeare also shows us murders committed for more complicated reasons. Ambitious people like Macbeth want to get rid of their rivals. The conspirators murder Julius Caesar because he is ambitious, while Othello kills his wife out of jealousy. Although he shows us why the characters behave as they do, Shakespeare usually makes it clear that murder is a terrible sin.

Murder most foul, as in the best it is;
But this most foul, strange and unnatural.
HAMLET, ACT 1, SCENE 5

Julius Caesar was stabbed to death by Brutus and other men he believed to be his trusted friends.

The ghost of Hamlet's father has come to tell him that he was murdered. Even worse, the murderer was his own brother. The ghost cannot rest until he is avenged. This became a popular theme in Elizabethan plays, where revenge was presented as an honorable thing. All too often, though, it just provoked more murders, both in plays and in real life. Many family feuds, begun with a single murder, went on for generations.

> *A bloody deed, and desperately dispatch'd.*
> *How fain, like Pilate, would I wash my hands*
> *Of this most grievous murder.*
> RICHARD III, ACT 1, SCENE 4

fain: willingly

Richard III has just had his brother Clarence killed—one of the many murders Richard has engineered in order to become king. Other victims include his two little nephews, the princes in the Tower of London. There were some famous real–life murder scandals at the court of Elizabeth I, one of them involving Robert Dudley, Earl of Leicester. He was the queen's favorite but very unpopular with everyone else. He was suspected of having murdered his wife, Amy Robsart, in order to marry the queen.

Richard III sent murderers to smother the two princes but made sure to stay out of the way himself.

In the world of Elizabethan court rivalry, stabbing or poisoning often put a swift end to a quarrel.

11

Treason

Treason was the crime of plotting against the king or queen. Because the monarch was believed to be God's representative on earth, it was like committing a sin against God. Treason almost always carried the death penalty. There were several attempts on the lives of monarchs in Shakespeare's day. In 1594, Queen Elizabeth's doctor, Roderigo Lopez, was accused of trying to poison her. In 1605, Guy Fawkes and his fellow plotters attempted to kill King James I. Shakespeare's early history plays, about the Wars of the Roses, include many treacherous attempts to overthrow the government.

Treason and murder ever kept together, As two yoke-devils sworn to either's purpose.

HENRY V, ACT 2, SCENE 2

yoke-devils: devils working together
either's: each to the other's

Traitors imprisoned in the Tower of London arrived by boat at "Traitor's Gate," usually during the night.

Henry V has discovered that three of his most trusted men have been conspiring with the French enemy to kill him. He has all three executed immediately. Queen Elizabeth dealt just as harshly with plotters in real life. When the Earl of Essex's rebellion failed in 1601, the queen had him executed, even though he had always been one of her favorites. Foolishly, Essex had announced his intentions by organizing a performance of *Richard II*, which shows a king being overthrown.

12

> *Though those that are betray'd*
> *Do feel the treason sharply, yet the traitor*
> *Stands in worse case of woe.*
>
> CYMBELINE, ACT 3, SCENE 4

Traitors were despised and feared by everyone. The Elizabethan government had its own secret service under Sir Francis Walsingham. His network of spies operated throughout the country, gathering information on anyone suspected of plotting against the queen. Traitors were sent to the Tower of London, where they could be imprisoned for years before finally being executed. Often they were tortured in the room under the White Tower. The only hope for anyone convicted of treason was to beg for a royal pardon, but this was rarely granted.

Supporters of Mary Queen of Scots's claim to the English throne were declared traitors. Mary herself was beheaded in 1587.

Prisoners stretched on the rack usually confessed or betrayed their companions.

As two yoke-devils sworn

to either's pur.

The Watch

In Shakespeare's time, there was no official police force. Instead, they had the watch—patrols of armed citizens under the command of a constable. As the first layer in the system of law and order, the watch kept peace on a local level. When members of the watch caught anyone misbehaving, they arrested them and took them to a magistrate to be questioned and dealt with. Members of the watch carried considerable authority, and because of this, they generally were feared and disliked.

The sheriff and all the watch are at the door; they are come to search the house. Shall I let them in?
HENRY IV, PART 1, ACT 2, SCENE 4

In this quote, the watch is pursuing Falstaff after a robbery. When a crime was committed, it was up to ordinary citizens to raise the alarm—the "hue and cry." This meant shouting and generally making a noise to attract attention. Everyone then had to chase after the criminal. The watch would take over as soon as it was alerted. If a thief was caught with stolen goods on him, he was convicted on the spot.

Although everyone joined in the hue and cry, thieves often managed to escape in the narrow, crowded streets.

Because there was no street lighting, the bellman carried a lantern so he could see and be seen on his night patrol.

> *You are thought here to be the most senseless and fit man for the constable of the watch; therefore bear you the lantern. This is your charge: you shall comprehend all vagrom men; you are to bid any man stand, in the prince's name.… You are to call at all the ale-houses, and bid those that are drunk get them to bed.*
>
> MUCH ADO ABOUT NOTHING, ACT 3, SCENE 3

senseless: sensible
fit: suitable
comprehend: apprehend, arrest
vagrom: vagrant

In this quote, Constable Dogberry, despite getting his words wrong, explains the duties of the watch. Most towns had a curfew, meaning that everyone had to be off the streets by about 10:00 at night. In London, the city gates were locked at dusk. The watch was armed with heavy sticks, a spiked pole known as a "brown bill," a bell, and a lantern.

The watch was made up of ordinary townsmen elected by the town council and responsible to the sheriff.

15

Justice, Law, and Mercy

The government passed laws to regulate almost every aspect of people's lives. You could be fined for not going to church on Sunday, for eating meat instead of fish on a Friday, or for failing to turn out for archery practice. People took each other to court for quite trivial reasons. Yet all these laws were treated with great seriousness by the courts. People began to depend on the strict definition of the law rather than on common sense, and this sometimes led to injustice.

Any accusation made against a person had to be proved in court.

fear: frighten
custom: familiarity

We must not make a scarecrow of the law,
Setting it up to fear the birds of prey,
And let it keep one shape, till custom make it
Their perch, and not their terror.

MEASURE FOR MEASURE, ACT 2, SCENE 1

The Doctor of Law, in his long, black gown, was a highly respected figure.

Because there were so many laws, people became experts at finding ways around them. When this happened, the laws were reissued and made harsher, as Angelo recommends here. Laws about public morality and those controlling vagrants were constantly being updated. Sumptuary laws, which said that only certain people were allowed to wear particular kinds of clothing, were revived many times since their introduction by Henry VIII.

The quality of mercy is not strain'd,
It droppeth as the gentle rain from heaven
Upon the place beneath: it is twice bless'd;
It blesseth him that gives and him that takes.

THE MERCHANT OF VENICE, ACT 4, SCENE 1

strain'd: forced

Not many real court cases were as grand as this trial scene from The Merchant of Venice, *but surviving documents tell us a lot about Elizabethan law.*

Shakespeare is more interested in the human aspects of justice than in the law itself. He says that showing compassion to other people is usually better than simply depending on the rules. In *The Merchant of Venice*, a clever lawyer tries to persuade a vengeful man to show mercy after he has won his case. He refuses but is punished himself when the lawyer turns the tables and uses the same legal argument against him. Elizabethan law could be just as strict in reality. If you failed to make your case against someone you had accused, you could be penalized yourself.

The Courts

The Elizabethan legal system was complicated and very strict. There were at least eight categories of law, and each crime was tried in a different kind of court. Simple cases like theft were tried locally by a justice of the peace. Serious crimes were tried twice a year by a jury at the assize court under a judge appointed by the queen. Anything to do with moral behavior or religion was dealt with by the ecclesiastical or church courts.

> *See how yond justice rails upon yond simple thief.... Change places, and, handy-dandy, which is the justice, which the thief?*
>
> KING LEAR, ACT 4, SCENE 6

yond: yonder, over there
rails: abuses
handy-dandy: make your choice

King Lear is saying that people should not take advantage of their position to judge others harshly. Through him, Shakespeare is arguing for a fairer society. Most Elizabethans were poor and badly educated. If someone was accused of a crime, he was compelled to appear in court at the risk of losing his house or his belongings. Every man was expected to know enough about the law to defend himself in court, but the poor were always at a disadvantage.

Justices also met at the Quarter Sessions (four times a year), where convicted criminals could appeal their sentences.

and beard of formal cut, Full of   wise

> *… And then, the justice,*
> *In fair round belly, with good capon lin'd,*
> *With eyes severe, and beard of formal cut,*
> *Full of wise saws and modern instances…*
> As You Like It, Act 2, Scene 7

justice: justice of the peace
capon: chicken
saws: sayings
instances: examples

Above: Mary Queen of Scots was put on trial at Fotheringhay Castle in 1586 after the discovery of a plot against Queen Elizabeth.

Lawyers and judges were always men and came from the middle or upper classes. Because the law was so complicated, it was a rapidly growing profession. By 1586, there were 1,700 lawyers in Britain. Lawyers were unpopular because they made a good living out of people's miseries and were suspected of taking bribes. After a rebellion in Shakespeare's *Henry VI*, the mob leader says, "The first thing we do, let's kill all the lawyers!"

The rather grand and formal Court of Wards and Liveries dealt with the inheritance of land.

Prison

Prison was not a punishment in itself. People accused of crimes were imprisoned until they were tried, found innocent, and released. If they were found guilty, they were kept there until their punishment could be carried out. Others were kept locked up because they were too dangerous to be on the loose in society. There were no fixed sentences. Anyone arrested for debt, for example, had to stay there until he could pay it off. Playwrights also found themselves locked up, usually because their plays were considered scandalous.

I take it, by all voices, that forthwith
You be convey'd to the Tower a prisoner;
There to remain till the king's further pleasure
Be known to us ...
HENRY VIII, ACT 5, SCENE 3

There were at least 18 prisons in London, each for different offenders. The Tower was for treason, Newgate was the main criminal prison, and Ludgate was the place for debtors. The Counter, open all night to take in people arrested by the watch, was usually full of drunken brawlers. The Fleet, the Marshalsea, and the Gatehouse were for better-off folk charged with crimes against the state that were less serious than treason. The Clink was mainly reserved for those suspected of being practicing Catholics, which was forbidden.

These prisoners at Newgate, arrested on religious charges, look quite respectable and have been allowed to associate with each other.

Most towns had a prison of some sort—a sturdy, lock-up building where prisoners were kept before being sent to the nearest city for trial.

20

Some of Shakespeare's Measure for Measure *takes place in a grim prison, with characters under sentence of death.*

> *I have been studying how I may compare*
> *This prison where I live unto the world ...*
> RICHARD II, ACT 5, SCENE 5

The most dangerous prisoners were chained to the wall by leg irons.

Prisons were cramped, unhealthy places with few windows and little fresh air. They were also expensive—you had to pay to get in and out as well as for lodging. The rich might have a room to themselves. The less fortunate shared with three or four others and probably shared a bed. Those who could not afford to have their own food cooked in the prison kitchens made do with charity food from the "alms-basket." These were bits of food collected from people in the streets and taken back to the prison all mixed up together.

21

Punishment

Most Elizabethan punishments were physical and rather gruesome. The authorities tried to make the punishment suit the crime in some way. For example, a thief could have his hand cut off, or someone convicted of slander might have his tongue slit. Anyone who refused to plead either guilty or not guilty was pressed to death with enormous weights placed on their chests.

... his father had never a house but the cage.... I have seen him whipped three market-days together.... But methinks he should stand in fear of fire, being burnt i' the hand for stealing of sheep.

HENRY VI, PART 2, ACT 4, SCENE 2

cage: lockup cage in the marketplace
methinks: I think

People had their ears or hands cut off or their noses slit just for stealing bread, let alone sheep. These injuries marked them as criminals. For the same reason, first offenders were branded with "F" for felon, like the person in this quote. Next time they were caught, they were punished more harshly. In London, felons were chained to the riverbank until the tide had washed over them for three days, which usually meant they drowned.

Hand-crushers were used to make people confess to their crimes or to cripple the hands of the convicted.

burnt i' the hand for stealing of sheep.

But methinks he should stand in fear of fire, being

*... I was like to be appre-
hended for the witch of
Brainford. But that ... my
counterfeiting the action of
an old woman delivered me,
the knave constable had set
me i' the stocks, i' the common stocks, for a witch.*
THE MERRY WIVES OF
WINDSOR, ACT 4, SCENE 5

Standing in the
pillory was even
worse than the
stocks, where at
least people could
sit down.

apprehended: arrested
counterfeiting: pretending, imitating
delivered me: got me off

The real penalty for witchcraft
was much worse—women were
burned, hanged, or drowned.
Women who poisoned their husbands
were also drowned, while male
poisoners could be "boiled in water
or lead," as one writer records. The
stocks were reserved for fairly minor
offenses like drunkenness, rowdy
behavior, owing money, or telling
lies. People were usually left in the
stocks or the pillory for a day or so.

Joan Prentice
and two other
women were
publicly hanged
as witches in
Chelmsford,
Essex, in 1589.

Shame and Hellfire

Public opinion was very important to the Elizabethans. The authorities realized that for most people, being shamed in public was sufficient punishment for minor offenses. People were paraded through the streets so that everyone could see and make fun of them. There was something, however, that Elizabethans feared even more than a public shaming. This was hell. People believed that hell was a real place where they would be punished for their crimes, even if they had gotten away with them on earth.

O, I were damned beneath all depth in hell
But that I did proceed upon just grounds
To this extremity.

OTHELLO, ACT 5, SCENE 2

were: would be
but: except
extremity: outcome

Othello has murdered his wife. His excuse is that he genuinely believes she is guilty of betraying him. Otherwise, he knows that he would be punished in hell. Many other characters in Shakespeare's plays also refer to hell, especially those who have committed murders. Richard III and Brutus in *Julius Caesar* both are haunted by the ghosts of those they have murdered, who remind them of the terrible punishment to come.

In the bottom right corner, damned souls are suffering in hell, shown as the mouth of a huge monster. Paintings like this were a terrible warning!

> *Fellow, why dost thou show me thus to th' world?*
> *Bear me to prison, where I am committed.*
>
> *I do it not in evil disposition,*
> *But from Lord Angelo by special charge.*
>
> MEASURE FOR MEASURE, ACT 1, SCENE 2

committed: put in custody

The scold's bridle was a cruel punishment for women, who were often accused of being "unruly" when they were really just speaking up for themselves.

Claudio here does not want to be shamed by being led through the streets on his way to prison. There were other ways of shaming people. Anyone accused of immoral behavior had to stand in church dressed in a white sheet. Women who talked too much or spread scandal had to wear a scold's bridle, a metal helmet that stopped them from speaking. In country districts, the "Skimmington Ride" mocked hen-pecked husbands. Villagers dressed up as the couple and paraded outside their house, acting out quarrels and beating pots and pans.

Villagers mocked their quarrelsome neighbors by making "rough music" outside their house.

Execution

Hangings were frequent and were carried out in public. They were not meant as entertainment but as a warning to those who watched. However, many of Shakespeare's characters joke about executions, suggesting that they were just part of everyday life and not particularly shocking. In London, the main execution spot was at Tyburn, where Marble Arch is now. The worst criminals were hanged until they were almost dead, then cut down and their bodies cut into quarters. After that the internal organs were cut out and burned.

Even the most skilled executioner did not always manage to sever the head at the first stroke.

... shall there be gallows standing in England when thou art king?
Thou shalt have the hanging of the thieves and so become a rare hangman.

HENRY IV, PART 1, ACT 1, SCENE 2

rare: excellent

As executions were quite expensive, local magistrates sometimes waited until they had several prisoners who could be hanged at once. Altogether, about a thousand people a year were hanged in England and Wales. Many others managed to get a reprieve by bribing the local sheriff, who was responsible for seeing that executions were carried out.

O Lord, Receiue my spirite.

In the 1550s, the Catholic Queen Mary had hundreds of Protestants burned alive. Burning was still common for religious offenses, as well as for witchcraft.

> *Some guard these traitors to the block of death,*
> *Treason's true bed and yielder-up of breath.*
> HENRY IV, PART 2, ACT 4, SCENE 2

Instead of hanging, aristocratic prisoners accused of treason usually had their heads chopped off with an axe. This was considered a privilege, a special consideration for their status. Some were allowed to substitute a sword for the axe. Henry VIII, Queen Elizabeth's father, ordered the execution of Elizabeth's mother, Anne Boleyn. Later, Elizabeth had her rival Mary Queen of Scots executed in the same way. The execution blocks were on Tower Hill and Tower Green, inside the Tower of London. The heads of traitors were stuck on poles and left standing on the south side of London Bridge.

In the Tower of London, the execution block and axe used to chop off the head of Anne Boleyn can still be seen.

Banishment

The punishment for serious crimes against the state, for anyone lucky enough to escape execution, was to be banished. This meant the convicted person had to leave England. Sometimes this was for a set period or, in more serious cases, for life. For the aristocracy, being banished from the royal court was almost as bad. When the Earl of Essex was dismissed from Queen Elizabeth's court in 1599, he immediately lost his influence in society and all his privileges. He was threatened with poverty and ruin.

> *Five days do we allot thee for provision*
> *To shield thee from disasters of the world;*
> *And on the sixth to turn thy hated back*
> *Upon our kingdom: if on the tenth day following*
> *Thy banish'd trunk be found in our dominions,*
> *The moment is thy death.*
> KING LEAR, ACT 1, SCENE 1

allot: assign
trunk: body

The Earl of Essex was handsome and dashing, but reckless. Although the queen pardoned him for many offenses, he eventually was executed for treason.

The Earl of Kent is being banished unfairly. However, he takes a great risk, ignores his sentence, and stays in England. He then returns in disguise to help the king who banished him. He also seems to have no family, which is good because banishment hurt the whole household. It interfered with the inheritance of property and split up husbands, wives, and children.

Romeo finds out from the friar that he is to be banished.

Ha! Banishment? Be merciful, say —
death;
For exile hath more terror in his look,
Much more than death. Do not say —
banishment.

ROMEO AND JULIET, ACT 3,
SCENE 3

Romeo has been banished from
Verona for killing one of the duke's
family in a duel. He has been
banished only to a nearby city, but it
is enough to separate him from Juliet.
This shows how much people feared
being separated from home and their
familiar surroundings. Sending aid to
a banished family member while they
were abroad was forbidden. Since
exiled foreigners were regarded with
suspicion, they therefore might have
no means of making a living.

*Banishment meant
severe hardship or
destitution for the
family left behind.*

Time Line

1533 Princess Elizabeth, daughter of King Henry VIII, is born.

1536 Henry VIII passes a law allowing the branding of beggars.

1564 William Shakespeare is born.

1554 Under Queen Mary, Roman Catholicism is reestablished in England.

1558 Elizabeth becomes queen.

1563 Laws are passed against witchcraft.

1572 A law is passed by Parliament for the punishment of vagrants, including traveling actors.

1576 An act of Parliament establishes houses of correction and hard labor for vagrants and thieves.

1577 Sir Francis Drake sets off on his voyage around the world.

1580 New building in London is forbidden in an attempt to restrict growth in the city.

1587 Mary Queen of Scots is executed after being implicated in a plot to kill Queen Elizabeth.

1594 Poor grain harvests increase the price of bread, the main food of the poor.

1596 Laws against vagrants are enforced, ordering the punishment of people with forged papers.

1597 A law is passed for the punishment of "Rogues, Vagabonds and Sturdy Beggars."

1598 New poor laws are introduced to take care of the poor. Another law places London vagabonds under martial law (policed according to military rules).

1599 Laws are passed against piracy.

1600 Statutes against vagabonds and the use of handguns are enforced.

1601 Poor laws compel each church to provide work for the unemployed. London vagabonds are again placed under martial law.

1603 Queen Elizabeth dies and is succeeded by James I.

1605 The Gunpowder Plot to blow up Parliament is exposed on November 5.

1612 Witchcraft trials in Pendle, Lancashire, condemn many women to burning.

1616 Shakespeare dies.

Glossary

Difficult Shakespearean words appear beside each quotation. This glossary explains words used in the main text.

assize court	The principal court in each county.
branding	Burning with a red-hot iron.
convicted	Found guilty.
felon	Someone who has committed a serious crime.
highwayman	A robber on horseback.
justice of the peace	A non-professional judge responsible for keeping the peace in his area.
magistrate	An officer concerned with the administration of the law; another name for justice of the peace.
malcontent	Someone discontented or at odds with society.
martial law	Law maintained by the army.
pillory	A wooden structure with holes for the head and hands that was used as a form of punishment for petty crimes.
reprieve	Postponement or cancellation of a sentence.
slander	Saying bad or untrue things about another person.
stocks	A wooden structure with holes for the legs and hands that was used as a form of punishment for petty crimes.
swindler	A cheat.
Tower of London	The royal palace, fortress, and prison on the Thames River.
treacherous	Likely to betray.
treason	The crime of plotting against the monarch or government.
vagabond	A tramp or wandering, homeless person.
Wars of the Roses	A series of wars fought between the families of York and Lancaster (1455–1485).
White Tower	The central building in the Tower of London.

Further Information

Further Reading

Childs, Alan. *A Day in the Life of a Tudor Criminal*. London: Hodder Wayland, 1999.

Chrisp, Peter. *Eyewitness: Shakespeare*. London: Dorling Kindersley, 2002.

Claybourne, Anna. *The Usborne World of Shakespeare*. London: Usborne, 2001.

Elborough, Travis. *Highwaymen, Outlaws and Bandits of London*. London: Watling Street, 2004.

Elborough, Travis. *Rebels, Traitors and Turncoats of London*. London: Watling Street, 2004.

Frost, Abigail and Mulherin, Jennifer. *The Best Loved Plays of Shakespeare*. London: Cherrytree Books, 1997.

Garfield, Leon. *Shakespeare Stories* (two volumes). London: Puffin Books, 1997.

Hart-Davis, Adam. *What the Tudors and Stuarts Did for Us*. London: Boxtree, 2002.

Ryan, Patrick. *Shakespeare's Storybook*. Bath, England: Barefoot Books, 2001.

Salgado, Gamini. *The Elizabethan Underworld*. New York: St. Martin's Press, 1992.

On the Web

For more information, use FactHound to track down Web sites related to this book.
1. Go to *www.facthound.com*
2. Type in a search word related to this book or this book ID: 0756508851
3. Click on the *Fetch It* button.
FactHound will find the best Web sites for you.

Index